St. W9-CSY-679 Library

Final Years of the American Revolution

Linda R. Wade

ABDO
& Daughters

Published by ABDO Publishing Company, 4940 Viking Drive, Edina, MN 55435.
Copyright ©2001 by Abdo Consulting Group, Inc. International copyrights
reserved in all countries. No part of this book may be reproduced in any form
without written permission from the publisher.

Printed in the United States.

Contributing Editor, Graphic Design: John Hamilton
Cover photo: Corbis
Interior photos: John Hamilton, pages 1, 5, 6, 7, 8, 9, 11, 12, 14, 17, 19, 21, 23, 24,
26, 27, 31.
Garry Wheeler Stone, Division of Parks and Forestry, New Jersey Dept. of
Environmental Protection, page 16.
U.S. Naval Academy Museum, page 18.
National Park Service - Adams NHS, MA, page 28.

Sources: Collins, Robert A. *The History of America.* New York: CLB Publishing,
1993; Carter, Alden R. *The American Revolution: Colonies in Revolt.* New York:
Franklin Watts, 1988; Charles, Carole. *Survival at Valley Forge.* Chicago:
Childrens Press, 1975; Gay, Kathlyn. *Revolutionary War.* New York: Twenty-First
Century Books, A Division of Henry Holt and Company, Inc., 1995; Grant, R. G.
The American Revolution. New York: Thomas Learning, 1995; Kent, Deborah.
*America the Beautiful: (*series*).* Chicago: Childrens Press, 1988; Lukes, Bonnie L.
World History Series: The American Revolution. San Diego: Lucent Books, 1996;
Microsoft Encarta '97 Encyclopedia; Old, Wendie C. *George Washington.*
Springfield, NJ: Enslow Publishing, Inc., 1997; Stewart, Gail. *The Revolutionary
War.* San Diego: Lucent Books, 1991.

Library of Congress Cataloging–in–Publication Data

Wade, Linda R.
    Final Years of the American Revolution / Linda Wade
        p. cm. — (The American Revolution)
    Includes index.
    ISBN 1-57765-154-5
    1. United States--History--Revolution, 1775-1783--Campaigns--Juvenile
literature. 2. United States--History--Revolution, 1775-1783--Peace--Juvenile
literature. [1. United States--History--Revolution, 1775-1783--Campaigns. 2.
United States--History--Revolution, 1775-1783--Peace.]

E230 .W28 2001
973.3' 3--dc21   00-056906

CONTENTS

INTRODUCTION

On a snowy Christmas night in 1776, General George Washington and his army floated from Pennsylvania to New Jersey across the ice-choked Delaware River. Early the next morning, December 26, after the 2,400 troops had completed the difficult crossing, Washington's army made its way toward an enemy stronghold near Trenton, New Jersey. The garrison was filled with Hessian troops, brought over from Germany to fight for the British.

The Hessians were in no shape for combat that morning, having partied the day before to celebrate Christmas. When Washington and his men marched into Trenton, the Americans caught the enemy by surprise. After an hour of intense fighting, the Hessians surrendered with 30 dead and 918 lost to capture. Washington's forces suffered only five casualties, with not a single man killed in combat.

It was an important victory for the Americans. Washington's army had lost several battles, but now they were encouraged once more. A few days later Washington's army marched farther north through New Jersey to win the Battle of Princeton. With these victories, Washington had driven the British from most of New Jersey. Only New Brunswick and Amboy remained under British control.

These battles proved Washington's ability to lead and win. In less than two weeks, not only did he liberate nearly all of New Jersey, he also revived the drooping spirits of the American Revolution.

A monument stands today in Princeton, New Jersey, commemorating General George Washington's famous battlefield victory in 1777.

CHAPTER 1

EARLY 1777

In early January, 1777, Washington's army marched to its winter encampment at Morristown, New Jersey. Now Washington had to deal with soldiers whose enlistments were about to expire. Also, because of harsh winter weather, many soldiers deserted and went home. At one point the patriot army shrank to less than 1,000 men.

When the warmer days of spring arrived, local citizens enthusiastically volunteered to fight the British. Virginia riflemen, known to be skilled sharpshooters, joined up with Washington's army, which grew to about 9,000 recruits.

In the meantime, the British had built up a large force to the north, in Canada. During late winter and early spring, over 7,000 British troops left Canada and entered New York. Their plan was to control Albany and the Hudson River, cutting New England off from the rest of the colonies, and hopefully crushing the rebellion.

Early in July, the British Army, commanded by General John Burgoyne, surprised the Americans at Fort Ticonderoga on Lake Champlain, in upstate New York. Fort Ti (as it is often called) was built by the French to protect the wilderness waterways used for the

A cannon guards Lake Champlain at Fort Ticonderoga.

fur trade. It was captured by the British in 1759, and then by the Americans, led by Ethan Allen and Benedict Arnold, in 1775.

During the 1777 campaign, General Burgoyne reclaimed Fort Ti by moving cannon high atop Mount Defiance, just to the south. Outnumbered and with a terrible bombardment sure to come from the British cannon, the Americans escaped during the night on July 5. With this victory, Burgoyne began his march south toward Albany, continuing his attempt to take control of the Hudson River valley.

A statue of John Stark at the Bennington battle monument in Bennington, Vermont.

Burgoyne found the going hard. In their retreat ahead of the British, the American forces carried away most food supplies, felled trees, wrecked bridges, and generally made the journey as miserable as possible for the enemy.

Expected British reinforcements never arrived; they were bogged down fighting at Fort Stanwix to the west. With his supplies quickly running out, Burgoyne decided to split his forces. He sent a group of about 700 men east to Bennington, Vermont, where the Americans had stockpiled military supplies, including food and horses. When this group of Germans and Loyalists attacked on August 16, however, they met fierce resistance. American General John Stark and 2,600 militia troops from New Hampshire and Vermont killed over 200 of the enemy and took hundreds of prisoners. A German relief force was also driven back by the Americans, with nearly a third of the enemy killed.

Frustrated, and now behind schedule, General Burgoyne continued his trek south toward Albany.

CHAPTER 2

DEFEAT AT BRANDYWINE

As fighting raged in the north, British General William Howe was busy with another plan: the invasion and occupation of Philadelphia, Pennsylvania, at that time the capital of the new republic. On August 24, 1777, Howe landed 13,000 British and 5,000 Hessian troops near Head of Elk, Maryland, at the upper part of Chesapeake Bay.

General Washington was determined to stop Howe's army from reaching Philadelphia. He placed his force of about 11,000 soldiers on the east side of the Chadd's Ford Crossing of Brandywine Creek, about 25 miles southwest of the capital city. At that time, trees grew thickly on the banks of the Brandywine. The only place to cross a large army was at a ford, a shallow part of a river where it's possible to cross by wading or on horseback. Washington believed that Howe's army would have to cross at Chadd's Ford, or a handful of other fords nearby, if it hoped to reach Philadelphia.

Washington's headquarters at Brandywine Battlefield.

General Howe, though, knew of fords to the north that Washington had left unguarded. He would not make a head-on attack against the defenses at Chadd's Ford. Instead, on September 11, Howe sent General Lord George Cornwallis and 13,000 troops farther north to cross the Brandywine. His hope was to then attack the lightly defended right side of the American army.

Steep hills, woods, and a dense morning fog hid the British troop movements. To keep Washington occupied a small group of Hessians attacked at Chadd's Ford. Washington at first was sure this was the main part of the British army. But as the day wore on, General Washington received sketchy reports of large British troop movements to the north. At first, Washington was skeptical, but once he was finally convinced of Howe's trickery, he wasted no time in moving his troops to higher ground. But by then, General Howe was ready to strike.

Americans suffered nearly 1,000 casualties at Brandywine.

At about 4 P.M., after successfully crossing the Brandywine, the main part of Howe's army attacked. The fighting was fierce. Outnumbered and outmaneuvered, the Americans were forced to withdraw bit by bit. Their determination slowed the British advance, but the redcoats pressed their attack. Soon the Americans were in full retreat.

It was an organized retreat, however. As they withdrew from the area, the Americans kept fighting. One unit especially, General George Weedon's brigade, delayed the enemy long enough for the rest of the Americans to escape. By nightfall the British, exhausted from their forced march earlier in the day, plus the fierce fighting, were forced to give up the chase. British casualties that day totaled about 600 killed or wounded. The Americans suffered nearly 1,000 casualties, in addition to 400 men taken prisoner.

Even though Howe defeated the American army at Brandywine, he was unable to crush it as he had hoped. He didn't expect the Americans to put up such a fight.

The American army's spirits remained high. The troops didn't think the defeat was due to poor fighting ability. Instead, they blamed it on a lack of knowledge of the area, plus poor observation of the enemy before the battle (reconnaissance).

Still, the British won the day. For the next several days after Brandywine, Washington and Howe's forces moved closer to Philadelphia, each army trying to find the other at a disadvantage. But no action was taken for the next two weeks. The Continental Congress finally fled the capital as the British drew near, temporarily relocating to Lancaster, Pennsylvania.

On September 26, a group of British soldiers entered Philadelphia with no American forces to stop them. The spirit of the revolution was hurt, but Washington and his troops were determined to continue the fight for freedom.

CHAPTER 3

PAOLI MASSACRE

Ten days after the Battle at Brandywine Creek there was another bloody encounter. General Anthony Wayne was in his home area of Paoli, Pennsylvania. Washington ordered him to use his knowledge of the area and launch a surprise attack on the British.

However, the British learned of the planned attack. They decided to attack at night, using only bayonets or swords. By not firing their guns, the British hoped to remain hidden in the darkness.

In the dead of night, the redcoats attacked. The alarm was raised, but the British began sinking their bayonets into the sleepy and unprepared Americans. When Wayne's frightened and disorganized men fired their guns, the muzzle flashes only gave away their positions. The British rushed in and cut the lines to pieces.

General Wayne and his troops were finally able to retreat. He prevented his four cannon from being captured, but 53 American soldiers died, over 150 were wounded, and 71 captured.

The way the British fought at the Paoli "Massacre" did not violate the rules of war. General Wayne's American forces were, after all, at Paoli for one reason: to destroy the British. But the hunter became the hunted in a very one-sided victory. To the Americans, though, the British actions were an atrocity, and only steeled the resolve of the patriot cause.

The attack at Paoli cost the Americans nearly 300 casualties.

CHAPTER 4

GERMANTOWN AND SARATOGA

After the defeat at Brandywine, General George Washington was determined to rid Philadelphia of the British. General Howe and about 9,000 redcoats were encamped at Germantown, Pennsylvania, just north of the occupied capital. On October 4, Washington divided his army into four separate columns, hoping to crush the British in a surprise, double pincher move. But the plan was too complicated for the poorly trained army.

At dawn the Americans, about 11,000 strong, marched into Germantown on two roads. The first attack succeeded in pushing the British back. But then a group of redcoats holed up in a large stone mansion, the Chew House. The American advance was slowed as they unsuccessfully tried to dislodge the British from the mansion. Fog on the battlefield added to the confusion. Soon the Americans were firing on each other, which caused a panic.

Washington retreated with the loss of over 700 killed or wounded. Over 400 were captured. Still, many Americans were impressed that Washington could rally his army and

Cannon overlooking the battlefield at Saratoga National Historical Park in New York.

attack so soon after the defeat at Brandywine. What the country desperately needed now was a clear victory.

Back in New York state, British General Burgoyne rested his army at Saratoga (now Schuylerville, New York) along the banks of the Hudson River. After three weeks resting and refilling supplies, he decided to press on toward Albany, New York.

On September 13, the British force met 9,000 Americans commanded by General Horatio Gates. The Americans had dug in (set up strong positions, or fortifications) at Bemis Heights, a few miles south of Saratoga. It was a place where the road to Albany squeezed between the river and nearby hills. General Burgoyne could either make a run for it along the river road and risk destruction from enemy cannon, or he could try to drive the Americans out of their fortifications. Burgoyne decided to go toe-to-toe with the Americans.

On September 19, Burgoyne moved toward the American strongholds. Just north of the American camp, at the Freeman Farm, the two sides met, and a furious battle began. For three hours the battle raged, swaying back and forth over the countryside. Just before the British line collapsed, a group of German reinforcements arrived, turning the tide against the Americans.

Burgoyne won the battle that day, but at a terrible price: the British suffered 600 killed, wounded, or captured. The Americans counted less than half that many casualties.

The British set up camp near the Freeman Farm, hoping for desperately needed supplies and reinforcements from New York. But help never came. On October 7, General Burgoyne tried again, attacking the Americans with 1,500 men. Once again the British were punished by American firepower. American General Benedict Arnold led a group of soldiers in a furious attack against the center of the British line. As the redcoats withdrew, Arnold and his men overran one of Burgoyne's fortified strongholds at the Freeman

Farm. Nightfall ended the battle and saved the British from a total loss that day. In fighting over the past three weeks, they had suffered over 1,000 casualties; the Americans lost less than half that number.

The next night, Burgoyne began a retreat northward, hoping to find safety at Fort Ticonderoga. But after a miserable trek through rain and mud, the British found themselves in a fortified camp on the heights of Saratoga. They were surrounded by an American force that had grown to over 20,000 soldiers.

Faced with such an overwhelming disadvantage, Burgoyned and his exhausted army were forced to surrender on October 17, 1777. His depleted army of about 6,000 men marched out of their camp, then stacked their weapons along the banks of the Hudson River. The prisoners were then taken to Boston.

Saratoga was important not only as a military victory, but also because it encouraged France to join the Americans against the British. France realized that the British had been dealt a major defeat. By spring of 1778, the French were an official ally of the Americans, and would give money, arms, and men to the war effort. Spain also began sending money and arms. The tide had turned in favor of the Americans. But there were hardships still to come.

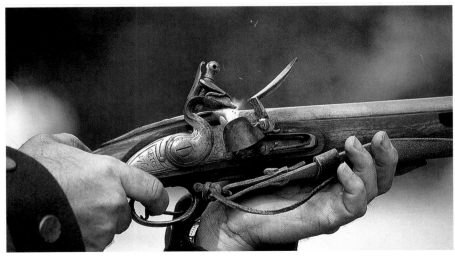

A close-up view of a musket firing.

CHAPTER 5

VALLEY FORGE

On December 19, 1777, General Washington moved his army to its winter encampment at Valley Forge, Pennsylvania. He chose Valley Forge because it had high ground that made it easier to defend. He also wanted to keep his army between the British forces and the Continental Congress, which at that time was meeting in York, Pennsylvania. British General Howe and his troops spent the winter in Philadelphia, warm and cozy just 18 miles away.

At Valley Forge, the American soldiers suffered in misery during the winter of 1777-78. Many went home. The men who stayed shivered under inadequate tents. The soldiers were often hungry as well as cold and sick. Their uniforms were tattered. Many had no boots; they lost fingers and toes to frostbite. Blankets were in great demand. Even firewood was hard to find.

But the winter brought a big change in the army. Up until now, it had lacked training that would give it consistent victories on the battlefield. Help came in February, 1778, with the arrival of Friedrich Wilhelm von Steuben, a former member of the elite General Staff of Frederick the Great, king of Prussia. Von Steuben was very skilled in military training, and offered to help the patriot cause.

Von Steuben developed a rigorous drilling system for the American army, teaching the soldiers to march in line and load muskets with precision. By spring, the Continentals were a well-trained army. Together with their new French allies, the Americans were ready to continue the fight for freedom.

CHAPTER 6

MONMOUTH

In Philadelphia, British General William Howe was replaced by General Sir Henry Clinton on May 8, 1778. Afraid of an attack by a fleet of French ships, Clinton left Philadelphia on June 18, intending to move his army back to New York City. General Washington and his renewed army left Valley Forge the next day in pursuit.

On June 28, an advance group of colonials under the command of General Charles Lee caught up with the British at Monmouth Court House in New Jersey. Lee attacked, but his orders were confusing. The assault went poorly, and Lee ordered his men to retreat.

Just then General Washington arrived and stopped the retreat. He ordered his troops to regroup. The training at Valley Forge paid off as the colonials repelled repeated attacks by the redcoats.

Redcoats firing their muskets at Monmouth Battlefield State Park in New Jersey.

Some of the heaviest cannon duels of the war raged across the battlefield. The Americans finally got the upper hand as night fell over the countryside. The British used the cover of darkness to continue their march north to Sandy Hook, New Jersey, where they boarded transport ships and slipped away to New York City.

The battle at Monmouth was a victory for the Americans. They had met the British on the open field and forced them to retreat, with casualties two to three times higher than the Americans.

CHAPTER 7

STONY POINT

Stony Point is a peninsula in southeastern New York that juts out into the Hudson River. The British had captured a fort on the peninsula in May 1779. They then launched raids against Connecticut coastal towns, hoping to lure Washington into battle. Their plan was to totally defeat Washington and end the war.

General Washington devised a plan. General Anthony Wayne led 1,500 men on a surprise midnight assault against Stony Point. On July 15, 1779, the men climbed narrow mountain trails leading to the fort, and then attacked. The surprise was a success. The heaviest fighting lasted only half an hour before the British surrendered. Fifteen Americans were killed, with 80 wounded. Twenty British soldiers died, along with several hundred captured.

The victory at Stony Point boosted American morale. Clinton's plan to defeat the Americans and end the war had failed.

Reenactors portraying American militia troops.

CHAPTER 8

CONFLICTS AT SEA

During the American Revolution, England had the greatest navy in the world. Instead of challenging the British directly on the high seas, the Americans began raiding English merchant ships.

John Paul Jones was a Scottish-born American naval commander. Together with several other French vessels, he raided the British coast, capturing many merchant ships. Jones' raids spread panic among the English. On the night of September 23, 1779, his squadron encountered a fleet of 41 British merchantmen, escorted by the warship *Serapis*.

At first the Americans took a frightful beating. At one point the British commander asked if Jones was ready to surrender. Jones shouted his immortal reply, "I have not yet begun to fight!"

Jones moved his ship, the *Bonhomme Richard,* so that its hull lined up with the *Serapis*, then lashed the two ships together. Hand-to-hand fighting raged across the two decks. At one point both ships caught fire. Finally, a grenade set off a thunderous explosion aboard the *Serapis*, causing the British commander to surrender. It was just in time; Jones and his crew boarded the captured *Serapis*, abandoning the crippled *Bonhomme Richard*, which later sank.

The *Bonhomme Richard* and the *Serapis* do battle off the coast of England.

CHAPTER 9

WAR IN THE WEST

Native Americans were involved in many battles of the Revolutionary War, usually fighting for the British. Even during the war, colonists were venturing farther west, often settling on Indian land. The British encouraged the Indians to raid white settlements in the wilderness.

Loyalists and Iroquois Indians massacred frontier settlers in Pennsylvania and New York. Many American troops deserted the army to return home to protect their families. Also, Indian farms were producing much of the food supply of the British army. In 1779, General Washington sent Major General John Sullivan to crush the Iroquois threat.

An Iroquois reenactor at the Battle of Newtown.

At the Battle of Newtown, in southwestern New York, Sullivan's army defeated a force of British troops and Iroquois warriors. Shortly after the battle, the colonial army moved north, destroying every Iroquois village and field in its path. Many Iroquois starved to death that winter.

In 1778, Lieutenant Colonel George Rogers Clark and a group of Virginia militiamen were sent west. They went to several settlements in what are now southern Illinois and southern Indiana.

In February 1779, Clark surprised the British and Indians at a fort in Vincennes, Indiana. The victory helped the American colonies win a huge area of land west of the Appalachian Mountains.

CHAPTER 10

CONFLICTS IN THE SOUTH

At the beginning of 1779, the British were faced with battle losses in the north, plus the entry into the war of France and Spain. The English formed a new strategy: they would attack the colonies in the south, where they believed a greater number of Loyalists would help. Once the southern colonies were under control, the British would push northward.

On December 29, 1778, the British captured the river port town of Savannah, Georgia, with 3,500 troops sent by ship from New York. Over 500 Americans were killed or captured, while the remaining forces fled to South Carolina. The British soon racked up victories in Georgia, the Carolinas, Virginia, and Tennessee.

Loyalists and Patriots waged a constant battle against each other in northern Georgia. Loyalists roamed the countryside destroying crops and burning barns. They also murdered men, women, and children. Patriot forces committed harsh acts against the Loyalists as well, such as at Kettle Creek, where 40 Tories were killed.

In the fall of 1779, an American force was sent to retake Savannah with the help of French warships. The attack failed; the French sailed home, and the Americans were forced back to Charleston, South Carolina. The British began a long siege of the city. In May of 1780, the colonial forces finally surrendered. The enemy captured over 5,400 troops, a huge loss for the Americans.

CHAPTER 11

BATTLE OF CAMDEN

After the capture of Charleston, the Americans rushed new troops south to attack the British. Commanded by General Horatio Gates, this force included 2,000 regular troops plus about 2,000 poorly trained militia from North Carolina and Virginia.

On August 16, 1780, just north of Camden, South Carolina, Gates' forces met about 3,000 redcoats commanded by General Charles Cornwallis. In a major blunder, Gates put his least-experienced troops, the militia (many of whom were sick) facing the best soldiers of the British. The Virginia militia soon fled, and the panic spread through the troops.

Gates' regular Continentals tried to hold their ground, but most were killed, wounded, or captured. Gates fled the battle in disgrace, his army in tatters with only 700 survivors. General Nathanael Greene replaced Gates as commander of the Southern army in December, 1780.

The defeat at Camden was one of the worst ever suffered by an American army.

CHAPTER 12

TRAITOR IN THE CAMP

The loss at Camden was a terrible defeat for the Americans. Soon they would be shocked again by the discovery of a traitor in their midst. At the beginning of the war, Benedict Arnold helped Ethan Allen capture Fort Ticonderoga from the British in 1775. Later promoted to general, Arnold helped lead the Americans to victory at Saratoga in 1777.

Then Arnold's life took another turn. In 1779, he married Margaret Shippen. He spent a lot of money on his social life, and quickly found himself deeply in debt. Arnold was also upset that he had been passed over for promotions in the army. He began writing to Sir Henry Clinton, the British commander-in-chief.

In 1780, Arnold was put in charge of the defenses at West Point, New York, an important stronghold on the Hudson River. He agreed to surrender West Point to the British in exchange for money and a position in the British army. Luckily, the plot was uncovered on September 23. Before Arnold could be arrested he escaped to a British warship. He was given an army command by the British, and was soon conducting raids against the Americans.

Eventually Arnold and his family left for England, where he advised the British on how to wage war against America. Because he was a traitor, he was never really trusted by the British, and was denied a career in the military. He died in London in 1801.

CHAPTER 13

BATTLE OF KINGS MOUNTAIN

Finally, a major southern victory for the Americans came at Kings Mountain on October 7, 1780, in York County, South Carolina. General Cornwallis was very confident after his victory at Camden, but the Americans had not given up. Part of Conwallis' army was a group of Loyalist Americans commanded by Major Patrick Ferguson. These soldiers roamed the Carolina countryside to hunt down any who were not loyal to England.

Patriot militia, many from the rugged mountains, fought Ferguson's troops on October 7, 1780, at Kings Mountain, South Carolina, near the North Carolina border. The militia charged up the steep hill, using the heavily wooded terrain as cover when the British fired down on them. Then the frontiersmen returned fire with deadly accuracy. Ferguson was killed in the fighting, in addition to over 200 Loyalist who lay dead on the battlefield. Over 700 were taken prisoner. Only 28 Patriots were killed.

British sharpshooters were no match for the Americans at Kings Mountain.

The victory at Kings Mountain made British General Cornwallis very cautious. He delayed further attacks northward, giving the Patriots much-needed time to regroup and rebuild their army.

CHAPTER 14

COWPENS

By the spring of 1881, General Greene still didn't have enough soldiers to attack General Cornwallis' main British army. Instead, Greene split his forces and fought the enemy using guerrilla warfare, designed to harass and slow down the British.

On January 17, 1781, a Patriot force led by General Daniel Morgan met a sizeable group of redcoats in an area just north of Cowpens, in northwestern South Carolina. (The town gets its name from the battle, which took place near a group of empty cow pens.) Commanding the redcoats was the hated Banastre "Bloody" Tarleton. In an earlier battle, Tarleton and his men had bayoneted 113 Patriots to death and wounded 200 others, even though the Americans had waved a flag of truce.

This time it was the overconfident Tarleton who suffered defeat. With great battle planning, and some good luck, Morgan outflanked the British on both sides. His sharpshooters and bayonet-wielding soldiers on the front line sent the redcoats fleeing in terror. At the end of the battle, the British counted 110 dead, 200 wounded, and 500 captured. The Americans lost only 12 dead, with 60 wounded.

American militia and regular army troops worked well together at Cowpens.

CHAPTER 15

GUILFORD COURTHOUSE

After the defeat at Cowpens, British General Cornwallis was determined to free the 500 captured redcoats from the Americans. He also wanted to restore British honor. He chased the American forces, still under the command of General Daniel Morgan, hoping to defeat them in battle. General Morgan played a cat-and-mouse game across the countryside of North Carolina, keeping his army one step ahead of the British. The Americans finally crossed into Virginia, an area Cornwallis wasn't prepared to go at that time.

After recruiting more militia troops in Virginia, Morgan went back into North Carolina, ready to attack Cornwallis' army. But on March 15, 1781, Cornwallis struck first.

At the backwoods county seat of Guilford Courthouse, North Carolina, Cornwallis and his 1,900 seasoned redcoats began a furious attack on the Americans. At the end of the battle, the British had held their ground, but at a terrible cost: one fourth of his entire army was either killed, wounded, or captured. The Americans suffered 264 casualties.

Even though the British had won the battle, Cornwallis couldn't continue on to crush the Americans. Instead, after two days collecting the wounded and burying the dead, the British turned and marched toward the Atlantic coast, eventually heading toward what would be the final showdown: Yorktown.

CHAPTER 16

SURRENDER AT YORKTOWN

The Revolutionary War had raged since 1775. The Americans scored crucial battlefield victories, but also suffered grave defeats. The battlefield wasn't the only place where trouble brewed. By 1781, the country was almost broke, unable to pay its soldiers or even properly clothe and feed them. The winter of 1780-81 was very harsh for Washington and his troops, encamped once again at Morristown, Pennsylvania. Hundreds of soldiers even mutinied, demanding pay that was owed them.

Despite the difficulties, for the most part the Continental Army had grown from a ragged group of farmers and shopkeepers to a well-disciplined army.

A cannon at the Yorktown battlefield, Virginia.

American and French troops forced a major defeat for the British at Yorktown.

In the spring of 1781, British General Cornwallis united with 5,000 troops led by the traitor Benedict Arnold. By August Cornwallis had set up headquarters at Yorktown, Virginia, hoping to stop the flow of American troops and supplies coming from the Chesapeake Bay.

In September, General Washington surrounded Cornwallis with about 9,000 American and 8,000 French soldiers. A large fleet of French ships had also set up a blockade at the mouth of Chesapeake Bay, tightening the noose around the British. It was a brilliant military operation on the part of Washington.

On October 9, General Washington himself fired the first cannon into the British defenses. With over 60 siege guns, the Americans pounded the redcoats for over a week. Several British strongholds were also stormed and captured by the Americans.

The British suffered over 500 casualties, with no hope for escape. Finally, on the morning of October 17, the redcoats were forced to wave the white flag of surrender. Two days later the troops marched out and laid down their guns.

The victory at Yorktown was the second time during the war that an entire British army had been captured. Even though occasional fighting would drag on until an official peace with England was signed in 1783, Yorktown would be the last major action of the war.

Chapter 17

Treaty of Paris

In Britain, people had been losing support for the war against America for some time. The war had grown very expensive, with British citizens paying the price in both money and the blood of their sons lost in combat. After the disastrous loss at Yorktown, the British Parliament began steps to make peace with the colonies.

On April 12, 1782, talks began in Paris between Britain, the United States, and France. Benjamin Franklin represented the United States at the beginning of the talks. Progress was slow, in part because of continued fighting between Britain, France, and Spain. Also, the Continental Congress had to first approve the treaty. Plus, there was no quick way to communicate across the ocean; messages had to be carried by ship.

On September 3, 1783, the final peace treaty was signed in Paris. England recognized American independence. At last the war was over.

Thirteen separate colonies had joined together against great odds to fight for their freedom and become the United States of America. But there was still much work to be done. As Benjamin Franklin cautioned, "You have a republic, if you can keep it."

Signing of the Treaty of Paris, September 3, 1783. Benjamin Franklin sits in the center.

INTERNET SITES

ushistory.org
http://www.ushistory.org/

This Internet exploration of the Revolutionary War is presented by the Independence Hall Association. Visitors can learn interesting facts about many aspects of the war, including major battles, biographies of important patriots (Ben Franklin, Betsy Ross, Thomas Paine, and others), plus info on historic sites that can be toured today. The section on the Declaration of Independence includes photos of the document, as well as bios of the signers and Jefferson's account of the writing.

Liberty! The American Revolution
http://www.pbs.org/ktca/liberty/

The official online companion to "Liberty! The American Revolution," a series of documentaries originally broadcast on PBS in 1997. Includes timelines, resource material and related topics—a potpourri of information on the American Revolution. Topics cover daily life in the colonies, the global village, a military point of view, plus a section on the making of the TV series. Also includes a "Revolutionary Game."

These sites are subject to change. Go to your favorite search engine and type in "American Revolution" for more sites.

PASS IT ON

American Revolutionary War buffs: educate readers around the country by passing on interesting information you've learned about the American Revolution. Maybe your family visited a famous Revolutionary War battle site, or you've taken part in a reenactment. Who's your favorite historical figure from the Revolutionary War? We want to hear from you!

To get posted on the ABDO Publishing Company Web site, email us at "History@abdopub.com"

Visit the ABDO Publishing Company Web site at www.abdopub.com

GLOSSARY

Bayonet

A sharp knife fastened to the end of a firearm and used in hand-to-hand combat.

Casualties

Soldiers either killed or wounded in battle.

Continental Army

The American army led by George Washington.

Hessian Troops

German soldiers hired by the British to serve against the colonists.

Loyalist

A person living in the colonies who remained loyal to Great Britain. They were also called Tories.

Militia

Citizens who were part-time soldiers rather than professional army fighters. Militiamen usually fought only in their local area and continued with their normal jobs when they were not needed.

Minutemen

American civilians who could be ready to fight in a minute.

Musket

A muzzle-loading black powder firearm.

Patriot

Americans who believed they had a right to stand up for their liberties.

Rebellion

An armed fight against one's own government.

A Revolutionary War reenactor prepares a cannon for firing at the Newtown Battlefield reenactment in Elmira, New York.

INDEX